MISS
THE CARRIAGE

To sweet Patricia.
One of the many gifts I have gained
from this retreat... meeting you.

Phil 3:10

MISS
THE CARRIAGE

SHANNON GALLATIN

· Foreword by Joni Eareckson Tada ·

REDEMPTION
PRESS

Published by Redemption Press, PO Box 427, Enumclaw, WA 98022

Toll Free (844) 2REDEEM (273-3336)

Redemption Press is honored to present this title in partnership with the author. The views expressed or implied in this work are those of the author. Redemption Press provides our imprint seal representing design excellence, creative content, and high quality production.

Scripture quotations marked AMP are taken from the Amplified Bible, Copyright © 1954, 1958, 1962, 1964, 1965, 1987 by The Lockman Foundation. Used by permission.

Scripture quotations marked ESV are taken from the Holy Bible, English Standard Version. ESV® Permanent Text Edition® (2016). Copyright © 2001 by Crossway Bibles, a publishing ministry of Good News Publishers.

Scripture quotations marked KJV are taken from the Holy Bible, King James Version, © 1979, 1980, 1982 by Thomas Nelson, Inc., Publishers. Used by permission.

Scripture quotations marked NASB are taken from the New American Standard Bible® (NASB), Copyright © 1960, 1962, 1963, 1968, 1971, 1972, 1973, 1975, 1977, 1995 by The Lockman Foundation. Used by permission. www.Lockman.org

Scripture quotations marked NIV are taken from the Holy Bible, New International Version®, NIV® Copyright ©1973, 1978, 1984, 2011 by Biblica, Inc.® Used by permission. All rights reserved worldwide.

Scripture quotations marked NKJV are taken from the New King James Version. Copyright © 1982 by Thomas Nelson, Inc. Used by permission. All rights reserved.

Scripture quotations marked NLT are taken from the Holy Bible, New Living Translation, copyright © 1996, 2004, 2015 by Tyndale House Foundation. Used by permission of Tyndale House Publishers Inc., Carol Stream, Illinois 60188. All rights reserved.

Lyrics noted in Chapter Four are from the Vanishing Point CD by Mary Barrett Copyright © Footstep Records, 3500 North Courtenay Pkwy. Merritt Island, FL 32953. Used by permission.

"It Is Well" by Horatio Stafford, Copyright ©1873, in Chapter Nine, is public domain.

ISBN: 978-1-68314-478-6 (Paperback)
978-1-68314-479-3 (ePub)
978-1-68314-480-9 (Mobi)

Library of Congress Catalog Card Number: 2017950139

Foreword

I have been married for 35 years, but never had a baby. I have never lost a baby. But I understand the overwhelming anguish of deep loss when your most cherished hopes are ripped from your heart. A broken neck did that to me.

One moment, my life was fine; the next, I was instantly paralyzed. I had to wake up the next morning and somehow keep breathing. I had to accept that life would never be the same. I had to learn to live with legs that did not walk and hands that did not work. That alone taught me much about grief.

It's why my heart goes out to anyone who has experienced a life lost. Especially the gut-wrenching loss of a miscarriage. Or even many miscarriages. For a miscarriage is experiencing loss at the deepest, most profound and personal level. Almost an impossible level, like everything inside you has died.

It's why I am drawn to my good friend, Shannon Gallatin. She understands pain and grief as few do. Through one miscarriage after the next, she has had to choke down loss like gall and vinegar. With a heart so wounded, so tender from constant bruising, honestly, Shannon could write the book on miscarriage. And she has.

But the small book you hold in your hands is not a sad recounting of one deep disappointment after the next. *Miss the Carriage* is a testimony, a personal journal filled with hope abounding. For when loss devastates your dreams, isn't that what we are all looking for? Shannon's book points you to the hopeful words of the Man of Sorrows acquainted with your grief who softly tells you, "Blessed are those who mourn, for they shall be comforted" (Matthew 5:4).

If you have miscarried a precious baby, there is a blessing to be discovered deep within the bruising. You *can* know comfort. It *is* possible. And over the next few pages, Shannon will take you step-by-step, inviting you to walk with her down the blood-stained path to Calvary. To the cross, a place of death… *and* a place of life filled with peace and joy that is out of this world.

Dutch theologian Geerhardus Vos once wrote, "What the Lord expects from us in seasons [of grief] is not to abandon ourselves to unreasoning sorrow, but trustingly to look sorrow in the face, to scan its features, to search for the help and hope, which, as surely as God is our Father, *must* be there. In such trials, there can be no comfort for us so long as we stand outside weeping. If only we will take the courage to fix our gaze deliberately upon the stern countenance of grief, and enter unafraid into the darkest recesses of our trouble, we shall find the terror gone, because the Lord has been there before us, and, coming out again, has left the place transfigured, making of it by the grace of his resurrection a house of life, the very gate of heaven." ("Grace and Glory: Sermons Preached in Chapel at Princeton Theological Seminary," 94-95)

Can the emptiness in your womb become a place transfigured? Unequivocally, yes. I am convinced *Miss the Carriage* will serve as a tremendous encouragement if you have struggled with infertility, miscarried in your first or second trimester, or delivered a stillborn child. Even as I write those words, I shake my head in sadness. When mothers lose babies, the pain is inconceivable.

But you couldn't have come to a better place than this remarkable book. You may think its chapters are too short to carry any real weight, but they are perfectly pithy. So please, don't plow through *Miss the Carriage* too quickly. Read its lessons prayerfully and act on Shannon's counsel intentionally. Next to your Bible, this small read is your best guide in discovering the hope that will carry you through.

So flip the page and get started. Get ready to move beyond the pain, even if just a little. As you do, may God's healing hand rest on you through every chapter.

Joni Eareckson Tada
Joni and Friends International Disability Center
Fall 2017

Contents

DEDICATION

I've yet to read a book or listen to music without noticing the names of people who were honored by the artist due to their hidden influence and valuable support. This small testimonial would never have been written outside the records of heaven without the indescribable love, support, and constant encouragement of the following people.

To my husband, Scott, who has been a constant cheerleader, an echo of God's love and grace, and the father of our seven children, six of which await us in heaven.

To my mother, who has shouted endless support from my life's bleachers and shared in my most valuable tears of joy and sorrow.

To my dearest friend, Linda, who has had the supernatural ability to push me outside of every writing comfort zone and clapped me over every hurdle in this process.

To my precious friend, Denise, whose meticulous skills of editing are surpassed only by her tenderness and compassion with every correction.

To a beautiful little boy named Toby. I never had the pleasure of meeting him, but his entrance into heaven just days before entering this earth, stirred my heart, surfaced memories, propelled tears, and provoked the birth of this book.

To a gifted pastor's wife named Angela. Thank you for the photo of the carriage on the front cover, which immediately touched an unspeakable emotion deep within my heart.

To my dear friend, Joni Eareckson Tada, who spent years mentoring me in the school of suffering and affliction through her many books and teachings, but now allows me the privilege of personal fellowship with her and her renowned pain pals.

To my wonderful church family and friends. There could never be enough pages to list the countless people God has used to bring value, wisdom, help and blessing into my life. I love all of you dearly and thank God continually for each of you.

And in everything I ever put my hands to, may Jesus, who has written this life story, receive all the praise and glory for anything honorable and good. I take full credit for all the mistakes and humanity.

PROLOGUE

Dear Reader,

After I had my first miscarriage, the last thing I wanted to do was dwell on the reality of what happened. If someone would have handed me a book on the topic, it would have found a convenient resting place behind bigger books on my bookshelf or a cozy corner of the trash can. I understand if you are tempted to do the same.

But in case you've come to the place where you need to hear you've not lost your mind, that someone else understands, that your emotional upheaval is not lifelong and your mourning is not terminal, then I pray this small compilation helps in some way. Years ago, I had asked my closest friends, family, and people I respected in the ministry if they knew of anything I could read that was similar to what I was walking through. There was such a loneliness to the pain I felt that I wanted some kind of companionship that can be found in another person's testimony. The only recommendations I was given were books on suffering with a slight reference to a musician's wife who had miscarried five children. The thought of swimming through two hundred pages of someone else's grief and repetitious loss was too daunting for me.

Then four years later, a precious friend of mine asked me if I could write an email to someone she knew who had tragically lost a baby. When I learned of her particular circumstances, I felt I had no words to give. I knew the Bible said to "comfort one another with the comfort" we had received, but it seemed arrogant to even insinuate that I could relate to her tragedy. I had only learned to "weep with those who wept" and wrap my lanky arms around broken mothers who craved to have their own arms filled with a baby.

Despite feeling inept, I poured my heart out in prayer for a woman I had never met, and then walked backwards in my thoughts to recount painful past memories.

My fingers began to type as quickly as my eyes began to leak and thirty minutes later, I gave birth to an email I never knew was inside me. As I sent it for my friend to review first, I prayed that what I shared wouldn't add any more pain to this woman's life. I admit to you that I feel the same way with this booklet in your hands. It is not meant to add any additional grief, and I apologize wherever my own testimony may interfere with the main message that is meant to break through.

I recognize that every story is different and how we deal with loss and pain is uniquely our own. But I learned in a deeper way, though no one else will ever truly understand what you are going through, there is a heavenly Father who listens to every heartbeat within you. From the moment He began to knit YOU together in your mother's womb, His main pursuit has been your heart; His main concern is who enthrones it; and His main desire is to take precious care of it for eternity. Though you may have lots of questions, lists of disappointments, and a soul that seems shattered beyond repair, there is a Shepherd who longs to heal, mend, restore, and comfort the deepest places of who you are.

I pray you have a greater revelation of His goodness and love through this testimony that I am finally able to share.

With much love and prayers for you,
Shannon

CHAPTER ONE

Rainbows to Raindrops

My first babysitting job came when I was nine years old, shortly after my parents were divorced. A single mom who lived down the street from me was desperate for someone to occupy her kindergartener a couple of hours after school until she got home from work. To a wise third-grader like myself, fifty cents a week was well worth my playtime.

When the school year was over, I retired from my lucrative career, but with a newly-planted desire to have my own children one day. That desire rapidly grew whenever I heard words like "You have such a way with kids!" or "Look, the children just flock to you." Then came the compliment, "One day, you're going to be a great mom," and my desire suddenly became a goal.

Whether I went to church, visited a neighbor, or perused the mall, I could easily be found with a baby in the nursery, donning puppets in a playroom, or making faces at little eyes hiding behind a parent's knees. In the midst of my own painful childhood, their innocence and harmlessness was like a magnet to my vulnerability. Everything about them brought joy and smiles.

At some point during my teen years, a brilliant plan emerged to have sixteen children of my own as well as run an orphanage. I read an article in a magazine about a family of that size and memorized how they put together meals, did laundry, and cared for one another. The picture of their joy developed a photograph of possibility in my own heart, and I set out to prepare for that day the only way I could. I bought kids meals from fast-food restaurants so I could collect the free toys inside. By the time I graduated high school, I had eaten enough Happy Meals to weigh five hundred pounds, build a playhouse with the boxes, and fill ten plastic storage bins with the toys and trinkets I had collected. It was a start.

But like most young people, I didn't realize the fallacy of the oft-quoted slogan, "You can do anything, if you put your mind to it." My mind had no control over the fact that I wouldn't fall in love and marry Scott until I was in my thirties. My strong will had nothing to do with avoiding infertility and barrenness. Sheer determination couldn't change the diagnosis that came from a doctor's lips after a milieu of tests and exams.

As my husband and I sat quiet in a near polar vortex, white office in the hospital, I thought it ironic that the walls held no pictures, the table held no magazines, and I held little hope of filling my arms with life. As kind and compassionate as the doctor was, no one can prepare a crib-craving heart for the words, "Shannon, I'm afraid you will never have children on your own, and even with our help, you and Scott will still need a miracle."

It rocked us both…hard. But only for a while because my husband and I had a strong relationship with the Lord. We heartily believed in a big God who laughs in the face of impossibilities and can create life just as easily as He created the galaxies. "He made me for children," I would think to myself. "He's just going to do a miracle by making me the mother of a small village for His glory." So we chose to walk the medical path as long as we had peace, and the attic became a holding place of hope with all my toy box investments safe and secure.

Then every sermon I heard, every devotional I read, all seemed to announce, "Here comes the first addition to the family you've waited for." We even chose the name Zachariah William Gallatin to be the name of our firstborn. "Zachariah" meant "the LORD remembers His promise" and "William" was after my father-in-law. We started to joke about our little "Zack attack" that would wreak havoc on our arthritic bodies, and if our first child was a girl, she best be a tomboy and like the stuffed basketball we already bought.

As fertility procedures happened and time passed, we nearly doubled the national sales for pregnancy tests. I learned that hormones are barbarous roller coasters that make Disney's Space Mountain seem like a speed bump. I also had acquired the art of mourning every time a dipstick shouted the digital readout "NEGATIVE" in complete defiance of my family dream.

At one point, the doctors had loaded my body with so much Clomid®, I produced enough eggs to birth half the amount of kids I wanted in a single shot. My mood swings had Richter scale measurements and were best described by one fertility nurse as "estrogen rage." "Honey, if you can get through this," she continued, "then menopause will seem like a hiccup in comparison." Since I was trying to start a family at thirty-four, in my mind, menopause didn't seem that far away. I laughed on the outside, but inside, nothing seemed funny anymore.

The days of waiting to see if I was pregnant crawled. There is a promise in Isaiah 26:3 (ESV) that says, "You will keep him in perfect peace whose mind is stayed on You, because he trusts in You." Well, I certainly trusted the Lord, but keeping my mind on Him looked more like mental gymnastics than a fixed focus.

One Sunday morning, about two days before another scheduled blood test, cramps came on suddenly during church. The pain was unlike anything I had ever known, and I ran to the restroom. Thirty minutes later, pale and covered in sweat, I found my mother-in-law, a retired nurse, and told her what happened. I knew I needed to get home and asked her if she could let Scott know. He was a youth pastor at the time, and I didn't want to interfere with his ministering to others.

As I neared the exit door, my mother-in-law stopped me and said, "Shannon, this isn't your period. You are having a miscarriage." Her words hit my gut like a sledgehammer, and all color around me began to turn gray.

I braced myself against the wall, got my bearings, and ran to my car. As I shut the door, I started talking out loud to the Lord. "This can't be, Jesus. You gave us a name. Rainbows of hope. You never break Your promises. No, no, no…" and though my words trailed off, my heart kept echoing as the evidence ignored me the rest of the day.

Somewhere in my heart, grief spoke, "Those promises were about the raindrops that make a rainbow...not a Zachariah."

Little did I know, that over the coming years, my own heartbeats would feel like painful contractions every time I saw a stroller, heard a child giggle, or smelled baby powder.

But the Lord knew...

"I can never escape from your Spirit! I can never get away from your presence! If I go up to heaven, you are there; if I go down to the grave, you are there."
Psalm 139:7-8 (NLT)

CHAPTER TWO

The Invisible Enemy

I never dealt with the reality of that first miscarriage. Instead, I did what I often do with things that seem too painful to handle: I moved on. I didn't want to think about it, look at it, relive it, grieve over it, or hear anyone else's story. Any of those options meant having to admit that I had lost a child. In my head, the words "lost a baby" and "miscarriage" were incompatible to the small gathering I envisioned clamoring for the last piece of pecan pie around a dinner table. I was going to have a large flock of kids that Norman Rockwell would have longed to illustrate.

Unintentionally, "barrenness" became an invisible enemy that seemed to stalk my thoughts. I kicked against the possibility of it harder than any opponent I had in martial arts. I didn't realize, until hindsight, that my normal desire to be a mom had turned into an "identity issue." My heart had grown tendrils that wound themselves around the need to be a mother, and my normal desire grew into an unmerciful idol. The innocent question, "Do you and Scott have any children?" had the power to obliterate any joy, anywhere, and during anything. Emptiness infiltrated the atmosphere of my life, and every Mother's Day was darker than Halloween. I'd dress myself in unseen mourning clothes of shame, failure, and self-pity.

Then, being a pastor's wife, I was very familiar with the curse of barrenness noted in the Bible. In the back of my mind, contradicting all of my knowledge of God's grace and love, I felt childlessness was what I deserved because of my sinful past. Of course, the Lord had forgiven me! Certainly, the Lord said I was a new person in Him, and my present life was made new as well. But in my thinking, I deserved the consequences of my present situation because it was

His mercy that kept me alive to begin with. I felt, without saying it, "I should just be thankful I get to go to heaven. I have no one to blame but myself."

Unfortunately, it would be several years before I would hear the truth found in Romans 5:20, "But where sin abounded, grace does that much more abound." Not knowing the power and freedom of God's grace, I stayed trapped as a prisoner to the whipping post of guilt and condemnation.

About six months after we let go of all the fertility specialists and doctors, I had an especially long workday that involved hours of travel in the car. The clouds in my heart eclipsed the beauty of the day, so I turned on a Christian radio station to vault my thoughts upward. Worship was a place I would run to when I felt anxious or fought depression.

Despite the upbeat lyrics, the music slowly began to dissipate as life's Master Conductor began to change the script of my thoughts. I could feel His gentle pull to share with Him the reason for dark overtones in my voice. Like music that gets into your head that you cannot shake out, the Lord listened past my words and wanted to change the melody He heard in my soul.

As I drove around the winding foothills of the Allegheny Mountains, the Lord wound my memory back through my past. Without permission, every facet of my desire to be a mom came pouring out, and I suddenly realized I was in such bondage. My fear of barrenness had strangled acres of joy the Lord had planted in my life. It hovered over my marriage like a blackened canopy that blocked any rays of light. So many years of spoken and unspoken pleadings with the Lord for a child turned into a convulsive confession of brokenness and enslavement. I pulled my car off the road and filled my hands, lap, and seat with hot tears and pleas for freedom and healing. I knew only the Lord could help me.

Just then, noted author and speaker Elisabeth Elliott came on the radio with her program "Gateway to Joy." She recounted treasures that came from Amy Carmichael's life and writings, especially pertaining to the orphanage she founded in India. Amy had become one of my heroes of the faith. At one point,

Elisabeth recounted that Amy made a tangible decision regarding marriage and children, and prayed to the Lord, "May my never having children here on earth result in more children in heaven for You, Lord."

There it was. The Lord handed me the key to this personal prison I was locked in. As my will surrendered and echoed Amy's prayer, I felt undeniable heaviness fall off my heart like iron chains. I realized the cleansing power of His forgiveness that wanted me set free from the infected clenches of bitterness. This fear I carried of becoming content without children evaporated as the truth of His satisfying love and companionship returned. There in my mid-thirties, the need to have a child melted into His grace and was replaced with a need to know Him more.

For the next seven years, my focus shifted away from motherhood and went fully into the ministry. I was able to laugh freely at baby showers, return to my old career of babysitting, and play peek-a-boo in public with other people's children. Psalm 40:33 says, "He has put a new song in my mouth—Praise to our God; many will see it and fear, and will trust in the LORD." My Master Conductor had given me a new composition in life, and it was filled with crescendos of freedom.

Turning forty brought on the reality of "aging" jokes and cards saying "Lordy, Lordy, look who's forty." Innumerable gray hairs ambushed my head at night, and arthritis became the constant reminder of sports injuries. I began to yearn for afternoon naps, and then something strange happened to my appetite.

As I opened up our fall women's Bible study, I made a joke or two about reading glasses, hearing aids, and the fact that Tylenol® and Tums® were now partners in my purse. The next day, after an oversized wave of nausea and four positive pregnancy tests, I wept as the hospital called confirming the news.

Eight months later, I delivered a little girl into the world, one week shy of my forty-first birthday. She looked nothing like a Zachariah but couldn't have been more beautiful to us both. My Italian mother-in-law had the idea to give her a good Irish first name, then a middle name after my own mother. Madigan Linn Gallatin may have been born into a pastor's family, but it didn't eliminate a temperament that created the phrase, "Madigan is mad again."

Though the pregnancy was easy, the birth was far from it. As soon as she emerged, eyes wide-open and a punch for the doctor, she was whisked off to the NICU with pneumonia and a plunging oxygen rate. In an exhausted delirium, I begged my husband to call people to pray. I had kissed the cheek of God's gift, and fear was pounding on the door of my attention.

An hour or so later, my husband wheeled me to the NICU, and I put my hand through a silicone glove on the side of an oxygen chamber that held our newborn. While I stroked around the needle poking out of her palm-sized head, the doctor told us that we almost lost her. Her oxygen had dropped down to 35 percent, and they had trouble finding a vein to get medicine into her.

"But then," he continued, "she suddenly made a turn, and we gradually decreased the oxygen until she reached 98 percent on her own. It's a miracle," he admitted.

The words "lost her" completely eclipsed the word "miracle." I stared at her, numb, unsure that we would ever leave the hospital with a baby. Fear peeked its head around the corner and crawled up next to me with all of its whisperings. I didn't like it, but I couldn't shake it.

Six days later, on Memorial Day, the warmth of the summer sun splashed across my face as the three of us drove home together for the first time. As I saw the hospital disappear in the rearview mirror, I exhaled a sigh of relief.

But inside, I held my breath and didn't know why.

CHAPTER THREE

TRUST BEGINS TO LIMP

Five months later, my husband Scott and I went out on our first "date night" since Madigan was born. Since it was our anniversary, we chose a fancy restaurant we'd heard about, and a couple from church offered to babysit.

I tried to remember what it was like to put on makeup and prayed for an outfit to adequately clothe an "over-forty-with-a-baby" body. An hour later, my face looked like a paint-by-number accident, and clothing couldn't cover the third trimester obsession with frozen custard. Regardless, as we walked into the restaurant, I let go of my pride as the darkness enclosed us both, and we ate dinner as shadows with voices. Afterward, we chose our favorite place to go—the largest bookstore in the city.

We always walked in together, but our interests would drive us apart until it was time for the checkout aisle. We gave each other a knowing glance, and Scott untwined his fingers from mine to head towards the computer magazines. I opted for the music section to see if my half-sister Melody had recorded any new CDs. She was an outstanding classical pianist, performing with the Chicago Symphony Orchestra, teaching at DePaul University, and applauded for being one of the top accompanists for flutists in the country. Sure enough, there was a recording I hadn't seen before, and I decided to order it online from home since the store didn't carry it.

Later that evening, I grabbed my laptop at home and searched online for Melody's latest CD. Rather than a discography list, web pages that covered her death and obituary from several months earlier unfolded before me. A full-length tribute had been written by the *Chicago Tribune* with notable musicians and opera singers reflecting on her life. The article said she had died from breast cancer, yet I hadn't even known she was sick! Words flooded my memory from our last conversation and the phrase "so tired" she echoed repeatedly took on new meaning. I could've kicked myself for not asking more questions. But questions as numerous as my tears would be given to my other half-sister Debra the next morning. Though I hadn't spoken to her in quite a long time, the fact she never contacted me broke my heart.

I woke hours before any rooster and percolated petroleum thick coffee. Though I tried to read my Bible and find comfort in devotionals, I gained nothing except a slight tic from incessant glances at the clock. Eight o'clock finally came, and I called the number Debra had for years just to listen to a disconnected line announcement. I grabbed my laptop and searched for a new number, and like a nightmare déjà vu, a page unfolded in front of me with links to Debra's obituary, posted three months before my sister Melody had died. I fell backwards on the couch in shock. Though I cannot go into detail, I would learn that her death was from horrifying circumstances.

Nearly catatonic, I called my only other sibling, Christopher, and shared with him all I had learned. Words were clunky and inadequate as we wrestled with hurt and confusion. There were too many unknowns for closure, so we ended the conversation with details about getting to our mother's house for Thanksgiving. She had been a widow for only two years, and a thirteen-hour drive for our family was nothing for us to be together, especially this year.

I don't know if it was a weird food craving or night sweats that rang a familiar bell, but on Thanksgiving Day, I started the morning with coffee and a pharmacy dipstick. Minutes later, I smiled as I held our six-month-old girl and announced that I was pregnant again. The news threw gracious light across the shadows of death that fought for a seat at our holiday table. As soon as our feast was over, we video-called my in-laws back in New York to share the surprise. Their spontaneous shouts and clapping amplified the joy we already had as we laughed end-lessly about nothing and didn't care.

I had no idea how this aging, arthritic, and bro-ken body would handle two babies at forty-two, nor did I understand why the Lord thought THEN was a good time to start adding to our family, but I made an appointment with the doctor and immediately changed my diet. Without consciously thinking of it, the camouflaged guilt of my miscarriage years ago made me eliminate everything that had the slightest tinge of potential harm. Since I heard negative things about caffeine, I looked at my addiction to coffee with disdain and embraced withdrawal headaches and cravings. Consciously, I was just being responsi-ble, but underneath, I was afraid of death.

One month later, on Christmas Eve, we discov-ered hormone insanity was caused by fraternal twins in my womb. I grabbed the side of the examination table and didn't blink while I stared at the two gray sacs on the ultrasound screen. Then at church on New Year's Day, my father-in-law dedicated our lit-tle girl to the Lord, and announced I was pregnant with "a couple of future linebackers." We all felt they were boys. Our SUV was traded in for a minivan, and plans for a double stroller became a triple stroller with an easy-pull hand brake, off-road tires, and the imperative coffee cup holder.

One particular January morning, I looked out the kitchen window, and beneath the typical gray of Rochester's winter, snow began to fall. I'm no expert in water chemistry, but there is a particular type of snow that looks synchronized as it descends in slow motion. Every flake falls at the exact same rate of speed and forms an icy soft blanket of white across the ground. As I watched, thoughts of the gentleness and goodness of God descended and blanketed my heart. "*Lord, I lost two sisters and now You've blessed me with two babies.*"

A few weeks later, I showed up for a second ultrasound shadowboxing discouragement. The first trimester nausea had disappeared, and the night sweats had dried up. As I lay on a familiar table, the technician searched for the first baby and found only a sac, while the second baby had no heartbeat or measurable growth. She looked at me sympathetically and said, "I'm sorry."

I left the examination room holding my stomach and praying for the Lord to hold me. On my way home, I stopped at the grocery store and mechanically threw items in my cart as I suppressed every urge to break the lights with a bloodcurdling scream. I couldn't shake the feeling that my body resembled a tomb rather than a cradle for my twins.

One month later, after a necessary D&C, I was told I had to go to the hospital and receive an injection because of my rare blood type and the miscarriage. After I checked in, I was taken to the maternity ward and asked to sit on a birth mother's bed that faced a stack of receiving blankets while the shot took effect. As I thought of all the places that could have been chosen to house this miscarriage medicine, the world seemed very cold, calloused, and cruel in its ironic choice. Then I thought of all the women who had sat in this place before me, yet without faith or knowledge of Jesus, nor hope of heaven. I found grace for the next ninety minutes praying for these unknown faces and those who would one day sit in this room meant for life, yet shrouded in grief and deep mourning. As I left the hospital, I thanked God for the assurance that I would hug my twins one day.

The next Sunday, I walked back into church and said hello to the nursery volunteers, kissed the head of a friend's baby, leaked a few tears on a friend's shoulder, and tried to do what I do…trust God and move on.

But it got harder. Trust and I both started to limp.

> *You number my wanderings;*
> *Put my tears into Your bottle;*
> *Are they not in Your book?*
> Psalm 56:8

CHAPTER FOUR

A BOMB IN ISRAEL

Some years, winter in upstate New York seems to linger until the kids get out of school for the summer. And so it seemed for this particular winter season in my life; it was way too long, intolerably cold, consistently dreary…and lifeless gray.

One March morning, despite the depth of sleep I was buried in, my eyes shot open and anxiety flooded my heart. I sat up in bed and started to pray for my husband and the tour group he had led to Israel a week earlier. For the last few days, every news channel seemed to broadcast violence and the threat of war against that tiny nation. I'm not, by nature, the nervous type, but today felt different. As I rolled out my pleadings towards heaven, I rolled my body out of bed towards the coffeepot and plucked a card randomly selected from a small bread-shaped box holding a row of Bible promises.

Our morning ritual is that whoever wakes up first makes the coffee, pulls out the cups, and randomly chooses a card to put on the lip of each cup. Then I take whatever scripture I've been given and read the entire chapter surrounding it as part of my devotional time. I filled my cup and looked down at the card I chose: "I will give peace and quietness unto Israel in his days" from 1 Chronicles 22:9. I smiled in response and my thoughts whispered, "*Thank You, Lord. I won't worry about Scott a minute longer. You gave me a promise to calm this anxious heart.*"

With pen in hand, I opened the Bible to 1 Chronicles 22 and began to read a familiar chapter. It records King David's preparations for the building of the temple in Israel and encouragement to his son, Solomon, regarding God's call on his life. When I got to my coffee cup scripture I was able to read it in its context: "Behold, a son shall be born to thee, who shall be a man of rest…and I will give peace and quietness unto Israel in his days."

A SON SHALL BE BORN UNTO THEE? Without a second's lapse, my thoughts argued with the scripture. "*That's not possible. Impossible! Why am I even thinking that way!*" As if engaged in some kind of argument, I listed all the practical barriers my husband and I had carried out to prevent another pregnancy from ever happening again. I grabbed my calendar and calculated that my physical danger zone was now, while my husband was halfway around the globe in "peace and quietness."

So I poured another cup of coffee and shoved the thought into the next county. "*Lord, please help me move on. Heal whatever's broken and balance my hormones before I end up in a hospital for nonphysical issues.*"

Two days later, I texted my husband that he needed to call me as soon as possible. Within minutes, a picture of his face appeared on my ringing phone. With one finger wrapped about my toddler's chubby hand, I walked through Macy's department store dripping with sweat despite my thin cotton apparel. "Yes. It's completely impossible and yet, I'm pregnant again. God gave me the birth announcement two days ago, and I didn't believe Him." I recounted to Scott all the reasons why this never should have happened, yet the scriptures bombarded me about a coming son. As we talked, nausea ushered me out to the car and hope opened its door in my heart.

When I finally called the nurse practitioner, I felt the need to tell her apologetically all I had done to prevent this and agreed with her concerns about my age and previous miscarriages. She calculated a due date with a question mark in her voice and scheduled an ultrasound to be done at nine weeks.

Each passing day, I rejoiced as I got sicker and thanked God for every hot flash. But fear and a familiar technician escorted me into the same ultrasound room where I learned of the twins' miscarriage. I couldn't turn my thoughts away from what had happened on that same table only months earlier. Then the loud sound of a rapid heart rate interrupted my memories, and a little form showed up on the screen.

I looked up at the nurse who smiled and said, "Very healthy rate: 164 beats per minute, and the growth measures eight weeks and three days, right on target with your estimated pregnancy."

Tears slid across my temples and puddled in my ears with salty wet relief. "Can you print out a picture for me?" There wasn't a frame on the planet that would ever be good enough to display the miracle of this child. After so much death, God did a miracle. He jumped our human hurdles, ignored my biological time clock, then made the birth announcement Himself. Not many babies get that kind of entrance into the world.

Still glowing with joy, grounded in assurance, and anchored in gratitude, I had no doubts this would be a healthy pregnancy, even though blood appeared a few hours later. It was normal to spot after an ultrasound. "A son shall be born unto you," the promise read.

I also had immovable faith despite an emergency room visit the next night and the doctor's doubtful prognosis. "Bottom line, Shannon, only time will tell. You have a fifty/fifty chance at this point. There's nothing more we can do for you here." As I drove home, I had no doubt, this time would be different. My womb was half full, not half empty!

I felt as though God had already given us a name: Adam Scott Gallatin. He would be a little "chip off the old block" that would run around my ankles, wrestle with his daddy, and tackle either of us when it was most inconvenient. God would beat men's odds and accomplish the impossible. He loves it when we trust Him in our trials, and I wanted to bring Him my faith like a gold-wrapped gift I could lay at His feet. So this strong will of mine grounded itself in trust and determined that it would not waver or doubt, despite circumstances.

I woke up at 5:00 am the next morning and rushed to the bathroom. I didn't want to wake anyone up by being sick. Then—despite the strength of my will and the fortification of trust—I could not prevent what happened over the next hour. I don't believe it will ever be in print, nor spoken, but it ended with a horrified scream into a terrycloth towel on the floor of the bathroom. My mind, to this day, cannot linger there too long.

I don't remember how or when I got to the kitchen table, but I sat stunned until my husband awoke. I whispered the words, "I lost the baby," and remember nothing else about the rest of the day.

The next morning, as I got ready to drive to an annual pastors' wives retreat, I texted one of my closest friends that I was going to come. Mary had miscarried her baby years earlier almost the same way I had just miscarried mine. She would understand, and I needed a safe place for raw grieving.

When I walked into the lobby of the conference center, the theme of the retreat was beautifully displayed across a banner to welcome us: "I Will Rejoice." As the opening session started, a pastor's wife began to teach from the book of Habakkuk and read these verses from chapter three: "Though the fig tree may not blossom, nor fruit be on the vine; though the labor of the olive may fail, and the fields yield no food; though the flock may be cut off from the fold, and there be no herd in the stalls—Yet I will rejoice in the LORD, I will joy in the God of my salvation."

The words, "LABOR of the olive may FAIL" hit my ears and ricocheted down through my heart in endless echoes. As "the flock...cut off from the fold" broadcast a picture across my mind of a helpless lamb, I squeezed my eyes shut and tried to think about something, anything, that would help me from running out of the room.

I met up with Mary after the first session and could only stare at her understanding eyes. After a long hug she said, "Shannon, I wrote a song for this retreat, but had no ending to it...until I got on the plane and began to pray for you. As I was praying, the Lord gave me the missing lyrics. When I eventually sing the song, I will point to you in the crowd and give you a special sign so you will know; the Lord gave me the ending for you." Mary was an incredible worship leader, gifted musician, and anointed song writer. To hear that God gave her words in this way felt like a love song from heaven to me.

As we neared communion the last day, Mary stood on the platform and began to lead us into a tender time of worship and quiet reflection. Then she stopped for a moment and said, "The Lord gave me a special song just for this retreat. I hope it ministers to you like it has me." Then she pointed to where I was sitting and signed the words, "I love you."

As the song began, her words seemed to echo the cry of my soul and tear-pools formed in my eyes. "When my heart breaks over and over. When my loss is too much to bear. Still I hope, for I know that You are faithful. And I will rejoice in the Lord."

The lyrics filled the room, and I found myself on my feet before an invisible—but real—throne of grace. Like a child to its parent, I stretched my hands as high as I could and sang at a volume unfamiliar to me. I had to make sure my Father heard me and then, maybe, He would pick me up and hold me for a while.

Somewhere in the divine realm, I knew the Lord was at work. He promised in Psalm 34:18 that He would draw close to those whose hearts were broken and save those who were crushed in spirit. I held out a broken heart for His salvation eighteen years earlier, but today, "crushed" seemed to describe it best. Though the Lord had spoken so kindly to me, sent Mary's song of comfort, spoken words of truth, and embraced me through the arms of others, confusion and trauma filled my mind and dreams at night. My faith was launched into a deep, depressive abyss I never knew existed for a Christian. The darkness felt touchable. The hurt seemed immeasurable. Prayers were inaudible, and my soul was inconsolable.

Yet, being married to a pastor meant ministry was not something I could escape. So the next time I walked into church, I slipped past the nursery and donned a veneer smile for any who made eye contact. I avoided all figures under four feet tall and used a side door to sneak into the sanctuary. I wasn't ready for well-intentioned people handing me scriptures like prescriptions nor sympathetic hugs wrapped in lofty Christian phrases by those who could not understand. The full pews only exacerbated my sense of loneliness. As the worship team began to sing, I only mouthed the words, afraid to put a voice to them in fear of falling apart.

I wrote in my journal, "You said You'd leave the ninety-nine to go after the one sheep that was missing. I'm lost, Lord. Come after me."

CHAPTER FIVE

The Valley of Sorrow

Second Timothy 2:13 says, "If we are faithless, He remains faithful; He cannot deny Himself." This is His promise. Our God who cannot lie. And over the next several months, I would take my dog on countless walks and find silence the only language I could pray. I leaned heavily into the assurance that He didn't need my words and interpreted all my heavy sighs, groans, and heaven-bent glances.

Many people never noticed the invisible mourning clothes I was wearing. There were good people that said thoughtless words and thoughtless people that said harsh words. I wondered how often I had been careless with my comfort and abrasive with my counsel in the past. At one point, a woman I highly respected in ministry sent an email and said, "Shannon, I think the Lord's sending you a message about trying to have more children." I nearly rubbed the ink off the letters of my keyboard as I pounded out an angry, raw response. Words about her callousness poured out like punches, and I soon lost all peace. I knew better than to use a person as a boxing bag, so I surrendered and deleted my response.

I looked out our kitchen glass doors at spring trees that had recently clothed themselves in leafy greens while tiny flowers scattered color all around the edge of our yard. The abundance of new life agitated me. I thought about the mama robin that made her nest in the support beams of our deck each year. It wouldn't be long until tiny beaks would pop over the rim of the nest and we would hear hungry chirps calling for breakfast.

Normally, this season would cause my phone to lose memory space from the photos I'd collect. But I felt like pain had become an unwanted, unshakable intruder in life, and it skewed my vision of everything beautiful. It began to subtly change my image of God and paint pictures of jagged edges across His ways and throughout my days.

The Bible says that Satan is a thief, a destroyer, and the father of all lies. He loves when a person has taken a hard hit to the heart and is deeply wounded. With incredible precision, he assaulted my faith with shots of doubt and discouragement, then pounded my vulnerability with dark insinuations about God's love. I felt a downward gravitational pull against hope and trust in the Lord.

One Saturday morning my husband looked at the dark circles under my eyes and said, "I'll take Madigan to Lowe's with me, and we'll have a daddy-daughter day. You go get alone with the Lord." Scott viewed trips to the hardware store second only in excitement to the Bass Pro Shop.

I threw my Bible and leather journal in the car and drove to the most tranquil place I knew. The village of Pittsford has a northeastern charm about it that's only enhanced by its rich history. I loved to walk along the Erie Canal, toss bread bits to the ducks and geese, and watch the fish snatch whatever remnants were missed. Copious aromas from a popular Mediterranean restaurant always filled the air and made the most satiated stomach rumble in greed. But today, there wasn't a single environmental treasure I wanted besides a somewhat secluded bench where I could pour my heart out to God.

I unwound the straps of my journal and the bindings about my heart and began to scribble abrasively across the pages. I had a healthy fear of the Lord, so I fought against the percolating anger in my soul, but the words of a trusted friend came to mind, "Shannon, God's shoulders are big enough to handle your anger and disappointment. What matters most is what you do with that anger and how long you allow it to stay. It cannot become a dwelling place."

Years ago, I had tasted what it was like to be filled with the poison of bitterness and have rancid words run past my thoughts through unbridled lips. Though it began as justifiable anger, over time it morphed into a self-deceptive character trait of bitterness with buttons easily pushed by others. Though I tried to contain it, the Bible is right in saying that bitterness will infiltrate, pollute, and defile anyone who allows it residence. It has no boundaries or restraints until it's repented of, cleansed, and purified by the Lord. The memories of those days still sting enough to make me afraid of coddling anger too long.

But I pressed my pen hard against the paper and engraved words I knew the Lord would read. I told Him that I felt like the news of this last baby's coming made my entire life clap. I had a picture in my mind of being like a small child with my heavenly Father, and as He clasped His hands around my wrists, He spun me around and around while I giggled with joy at His miracle. But then, while I laughed, He let go of my hands and I found myself on the ground, in deep pain, with His Presence nowhere to be found. Children trust their parents not to let go of them, but my trust was as wounded as I felt. I wrote how prayer felt like a monologue, grief found no comfort, and confusion battled my knowledge of truth. I was ashamed to feel this way as a Christian, especially being married to a pastor. Part of me was especially fearful of stumbling someone else's faith if they had a glimpse of how much I struggled inside.

Glancing at my watch, I closed the journal and looked out across the canal. A mother duck with feathery ducklings made ripples across the water as they swam towards the children along the shore. I whispered out loud through tears that dripped across my lips, "I have spoken to so many women about Your love, Your goodness, Your faithfulness. For years, You've shown me how You draw near to the brokenhearted, but this time, it feels like You were the one Who broke me."

My words trailed off, and I wept hard. There was no dignity left to shield my face from others who walked past. I strained to hear the slightest word from heaven and groped for any impression the Lord might send for relief. But the sun kept shining, birds kept chirping, children kept laughing, and no words came to my thoughts.

In the days that followed, I wondered if I had done something wrong. The need to understand robbed me of sleep. The questions in my head were like a rolodex: "Why did You create life just to take it? I know You're a better parent. I know the children are in a better place. But what was the point?"

My husband would try to offer comfort, but the grief seemed too complicated. One afternoon as I washed dishes, he wrapped his arms around me and said, "Shannon, some people's 'valley of the shadow of death' is longer than others. Only the Lord knows how long yours is. He is leading you through it, and He will lead you out of it."

I knew he was reminding me of the precious promises from Psalm 23. His words echoed for a time and offered a bit of solace. But the avalanche of my unspoken questions would often bury any rock of truth offered. The sense of being a perpetual victim of grief was amplified by counting losses rather than blessings. My losses had faces, names, emotions, and memories attached, while blessings felt numb, empty, and distanced.

God's tender compassion and mercy were eclipsed by mothers I encountered who didn't want children or constantly complained about them. Whether in a store, post office, or parking lot, I couldn't escape their hateful words or frustrated screams. News reports of abuse or abortion made me weep, and I'd battle the obvious, "Lord, why would You give THEM children?"

But this Father of mine is patient, and He began to echo a promise to me I couldn't escape. Whether I picked up a devotional, surfed the web, listened to the radio, or talked with a friend, words from Hosea 2 would somehow emerge: "I will give her her vineyards (fruit with joyful, medicinal possibility) from there, and the Valley of Achor (trouble or weeping) as a door of hope; she shall sing there, as in the days of her youth, as in the day when she came up from the land of Egypt."

I had no idea how the Lord could open any "door of hope" in my own death valley—full of shadows, tears, and trouble—much less fill my mouth with a song equal to the joy I knew when I was saved "from the land of Egypt."

Then light began to slip past the drawn shades of my thoughts, and I remembered life before Jesus. It was a valley of death with different landscapes, full of the shadows of suicide, debris from addictions and carcasses of relationships I killed in my sin. In one unforgettable day, Jesus had plucked me from that spiritual death, filled me with His life, and put a new song in my mouth. I sang it to anyone who would listen. But now, in this valley of trouble, the Lord was telling me that there was a door I did not yet see. In this place of tears, hope would open and give entrance to a new song, filled with lyrics of light and life that point to my Redeemer, Deliverer, and Savior.

CHAPTER SIX

The Door of Hope

Spring quickly turned to summer, and a perfectly sunny morning invited some sort of outdoor excursion. Though my little girl had turned one already, she still kicked against walking, so I pulled out our knobby-tire, cross-country, made-for-dirt stroller. I had yet to achieve the mountaineering mama status portrayed on the front of the box, but I could hike with the best of them. It would be a great day to battle some loathsome spiders and get cut up by thorns just so I could grab a few handfuls of ripe berries along a park path close by. I would wear my maternal scabs like a badge of honor.

Since Madigan slept in later than usual, I grabbed my Bible and opened up to read Psalm 16.

I had made a note next to it several months earlier when my missionary friend from England had called and insisted that the Lord wanted me to read it. At the time, I had just returned from the pastors' wives retreat and raw grief made everyone's words empty. Even the Bible seemed to be little more than black letters on white pages. Proverbs 13:12 says, "Hope deferred makes the heart sick," and I certainly was living out this truth.

But with the memory of Nancy's words, I began to read the psalm with renewed curiosity. This time there were no lifeless letters, and the words sprang to life and seemed to leap off the pages. Without conscious thought, I pulled out my concordance and began to read each verse slowly. As the writer proclaimed his love for God, he repeated the fact that his voice and prayers had been heard. Then in verses 3 and 4, "The sorrows of death compassed me and the pains of hell got hold upon me; I found trouble and sorrow. Then I called upon the name of the LORD: O LORD, I implore You, deliver my soul!"

I felt as though the Bible was speaking nearly audibly. I used my computer and pulled up a different translation of the psalm and read, "The cords of death entangled me, the anguish of the grave came over me; I was overcome by distress and sorrow. Then I called on the name of the LORD: 'LORD, save me!' Thousands of years ago, someone else was in the same place I was, saying the same words I had, feeling the same way I did, yet in different circumstances!

I went back to my concordance and looked up the word "sorrow." It wasn't an adjective or a verb, but a noun. What? How can my emotion be a "person, place, or thing?" Yet, my sorrow did have a face ultimately. They were people whose eyes I could remember or whose form I embraced through an ultrasound.

More than that, though, the Hebrew word in context meant to "labor in childbirth; to bring forth with pain." When you add that kind of sorrow to the word 'death,' it's a picture of a miscarriage. I sat stunned. The "sorrows of death" literally means that the labor pain of childbirth has brought forth death.

No wonder the next verse echoed my agony of not being able to deliver life, so I begged the Lord to save me! Save my heart! Save my joy! Save my soul! The psalm goes on to speak of God's grace and mercy, His help and ability to deal abundantly with one so devastated. Then came a promise in verses 8 and 9. This time, I couldn't HELP but to believe it. Faith flooded over me as I read the words,

> "For you, LORD, have delivered me from death,
> my eyes from tears,
> my feet from stumbling,
> that I may walk before the LORD
> in the land of the living."

That word "living" in the Hebrew means "to be revived from sickness, death, or discouragement." And there came a loud creak in my soul as the door of hope swung wide open on its hinges and God's light poured in. I knew there would be a day when I would walk before the Lord and His people, revived in my soul from heart sickness and grief that came from all of this death in my life.

So I did what verse 17 instructed: "I will offer to You the sacrifice of thanksgiving, And will call upon the name of the LORD." Somewhere inside, I exhaled. That breath that I had held inwardly, while driving away from the hospital with Madigan, finally released its stronghold, and peace replaced resident fear. My Father had spoken, and the eyes of my heart looked out the window of my soul as I began to look for Him again.

A familiar cry came down the hallway, and joy painted a smile across my face. If my child's cry to be picked up and fed moved me to respond, how much more did my pain-filled cry to be picked up and comforted move my heavenly Father?

With a backpack, garden gloves, and a Bernese Mountain dog in tow, I walked out the door to go berry picking and don heroism against all those cursed arachnids. *National Geographic* was NOT a good idea for me as a child.

As I turned the key in the ignition, I turned up the volume on a worship CD and never entertained a single thought that loss was not over.

CHAPTER SEVEN

LEARNING HOW TO RUN

I had heard of my OB/Gyn long before I ever became her patient. Her license plate said Mom1Dr2. It was an unspoken announcement that she considered motherhood her top priority and medicine second. She would see patients only a few days a week, and yet I never heard a single complaint from anyone. In each of her examination rooms, she proudly displayed the childhood pictures of her biological twins or black-haired triplet boys. Each picture perfectly portraying imaginations that conquered kingdoms, swung high from strong tree limbs, or giggled waist deep in bubble baths.

Midsummer had arrived, and I received a call that the doctor wanted me to come in for an exam.

I wanted to put all things associated with babies behind me, but a barrage of "worst case scenarios" spoken by her assistant forced me to relent. Despite the many months that had passed since the last miscarriage, my hormones were still erratic, and she insisted on lab work and a consultation.

I mindlessly made my way to the office and sat beneath ceiling tiles I had counted too often. A nurse soon escorted me back to a room where I slumped into a plastic chair adjacent the doctor's desk and leaned limp against it. I avoided all the children's photographs and traced circles across the desk's wood grain patterns.

"Ah, Shannon," my doctor said with outstretched hand. "I have to say, I'm sorry to see you again." If I had not miscarried, my appointment would have been with a nurse practitioner. "How ya' doin'?"

I smiled in defiance for about two seconds, then tears started to leak everywhere. My doctor had openly told me she wasn't a Christian, and I wanted to be a good witness, yet I struggled with what that looked like in my situation. I thought I would blemish God's name by being so emotionally broken. I prayed God would guard my speech, but I couldn't hold back the truth of the pain I still felt.

She reached across the desk and covered my hand with her own. "Shannon, let me tell you something. Out of all my years in practice, I see two kinds of women. Those who have never had children and miscarry a baby, and those who have had a child of their own, then miscarry later. Both go through incredible pain and handle it in very different ways. But you… you always wanted children. You thought you'd never have any and you worked through it. Then you did have one and it's more of a joy than you ever imagined." She leaned closer and said, "Now, when you lose a child, you really *know* what you've lost, and it cuts even deeper. Most women seem to have a much harder time with miscarriage AFTER they have already had a child."

The tear leakage turned into one steady stream of emotional release as she effectually validated my inward struggle and blanketed my wounds with understanding. I nodded my head "yes" and listened further to words I can no longer remember. But what a good God, to use an unbelieving gynecologist as a heart doctor for me.

I did not know how, when, where, or what the Lord would use to help restore color to these monochrome days, or infuse light over the blackness and shadows. But I wrote in my journal, "If all I ever know is a God that answers every time I call, or grants a 'sense of His Presence' whenever I'm struggling or lonely; or if I always feel immediate relief from depression with instant help through my whispers of neediness, then what a monstrous burden I would place on others when I shared from my lopsided experience of His ways!" I would pull out promises, like a doctor doles out prescriptions, and instruct "take these two scriptures and you'll feel better in the morning." What condemnation and further discouragement I would heap on the hurting!

It wasn't just one scripture, one book, one conversation, or a sermon. There weren't miraculous events or skywriting that appeared from heaven. There were no easy answers nor esoteric feelings of warmth like

God's embrace. But somehow, slowly, the Lord faithfully worked in my heart and began to fulfill His promise from Psalm 23:3, "He restores my soul."

The ministry continued on while I began to teach the women's Bible study in the fall and focus on day-to-day responsibilities. As I stayed in the Word and came upon promises that were hard to believe, I would wrap my arms around them and run to the Lord in prayer. His throne of grace was the best location to leave all of my fears, misunderstandings, questions, and requests.

I used to run track in high school, and a life lesson I gained was the power of seeing the finish line. Despite screaming muscles and throbbing pain, one glimpse would infuse a surreal push to reach the goal. Likewise, one small glimpse in my mind's eye of that place of grace with the Lord was all I needed to boost my spirit to run hard to Him. My silence in prayer from the year before was replaced with a constant stream of petitions, pleadings, and praise.

More weeks passed, and as I filled out a registration form for an upcoming conference in October, it hit me that I hadn't had my period yet. We could not afford the surgery to prevent pregnancy, but certainly did almost everything we could to prevent it.

Regardless, the digital word PREGNANT displayed itself across a stick in my hand, and I dropped my head in disbelief. "Oh, Lord. Am I going to lose baby number five? What in the world do I do now?"

And normally by this time, fear, dread, sorrow, hope, excitement, and shame would all be vying for dominance. But I felt only peace. There were no bitter barbs trying to choke my faith, nor scriptures that seemed to indicate what was about to happen. I just felt enfolded within a blanket of divine, inexplicable peace. A peace so strong that it seemed to roll out a blood-stained carpet of trust in the Lord, no matter the outcome.

CHAPTER EIGHT

TEARS AND TREASURES IN HEAVEN

Life was going at such a whirlwind pace, I never fully embraced the reality that I was pregnant again. Within a few weeks of the revelation, I was getting off a plane in southern California, driving along the coast towards the conference center, then wrapping my arms around my mother-in-law, Rosemary, who had arrived a few days earlier. I looked into her hazel eyes, encased by the yellow that came from her liver disease, and suppressed the news of my pregnancy. The conference was another gift to my weariness, and the sessions were filled with life-giving words.

About the fourth day into the conference, I began to bleed and conceded to another homecoming for heaven. My precious friend Kathy O. asked me if I'd like to walk around the tropical beauty of the grounds, and her companionship was more medicinal than the sulfur springs that flowed along the walkways. As I boarded a plane home the next day, I set my heart to auto-pilot, my mind to ministry issues, and disengaged all emotions from processing another loss.

The next month, the Lord delivered my dear friend Mary from her cancer-filled body and released her from the pain of this world. I can't describe the mixture of joy and sorrow, but I can attest to the sweetness of the verse found in Philippians 3 that I have claimed for my own in life. As a baby Christian, I prayed verse 10 would be my perpetual "finish line" that pushed me ever forward, "That I may know Him and the power of His resurrection, and the fellowship of His sufferings, being conformed to His death." At a new depth, I was learning the reality and sufficiency of Christ's fellowship that comes from His sufferings. What used to be a mystery for so long was now as tangible as the air I breathed.

There is a promise that a Christian inherits from Isaiah 61:3: "To all who mourn...he will give a crown of beauty for ashes, a joyous blessing instead of mourning, festive praise instead of despair. In their righteousness, they will be like great oaks that the Lord has planted for his own glory." During these days, from the time I woke up to the time I went back to bed, I felt a weight from mourning and grief, yet I also believed that He promised some sort of crown, joy, blessing, and a mouth that would be filled with praise. I didn't know when it would come, or how He would do it, but I had an anchor of hope for my soul.

Psalm 22 took on new meaning as well. To realize that David was allowed to feel such heartache that he would write the words, "My God, my God, why have you abandoned me? Why are you so far away when I groan for help? Every day I call to you, my God, but you do not answer. Every night I lift up my voice, but I find no relief." If someone like David, a man after God's own heart, felt abandoned by God and was met with silence from heaven and no response to his pain, then I was not alone. Then to realize that

Jesus felt this way and spoke these exact same words on the cross healed a deep place in my lack of understanding.

There came a beautiful Sunday afternoon, almost half a year later, when my husband and I packed up the stroller, our toddler, and headed over to Pittsford. We walked along the canal, and I soon pined in a pottery store, lingered in the leather shop, and inhaled those delicious Mediterranean aromas. When I glanced further down the walkway, I stared at "my bench." That place where, the year before, I flooded the grass with my tears and bled through my pen, scribbling out words from a devastated soul.

As I remembered that scene so vividly, I thanked the Lord that His black pit deliverance didn't come immediately. It came subtly and quietly without answers to questions nor understanding of His purpose. As the sidewalk began to be cluttered with bikers, skaters, and ducks eating scattered corn from charitable tossers, I prayed, "Lord, I still don't know why You were so quiet that day. I don't know if I've ever been that broken and desperate before. And though I don't need to know now…" but the Lord interrupted my prayer with His own response.

I immediately had a vision of myself sitting on that bench alone, crying. Then I saw the back of a form sitting next to me and knew it was Jesus. He had enfolded me completely in His arms. Next came gentle words to my thoughts, "Where was I, Shannon? I was weeping with you as you wept. I held you together while you were falling apart. I am your Friend that sticks closer than a brother."

I thought I needed His words then. I thought I needed His voice. I believed it was the time for Him to give me answers and understanding. But He loved me enough to not respond to what I thought I needed, but to meet the deepest desire of my heart, to know Him better, to have the peace that comes with no understanding. And despite my unvoiced accusations of His apathy, He held me that day; He held and understood.

Unknowingly, I had stopped pushing the stroller, and my eyes were glued in the distance.

"Are you okay?" My husband's words snapped me back to reality. Melted butter had more consistency than I did at that moment. As I began to cry, Scott said, "Oh no!" and rushed toward me. But I stuck my hand out and smiled and said, "Happy tears. This time…these are happy tears," and pulled out my Kleenex.

CHAPTER NINE

LIVING OUT ESTHER

Most of the people in our church knew that over the next year, we would lose our sixth child, my dearly loved mother-in-law, and my uncle. Each of them had unique circumstances but all were filed under the category of "loss." Since several years have passed since the last death, and for the sake of brevity of the book, I would rather pluck out a few of the "treasures of darkness and the riches in secret places" that He has graciously given us along the way (Isaiah 45:3).

One of the most significant jewels came during this sixth pregnancy. I was about nine weeks along and had begun to spot a few days before leaving to teach a women's retreat. The conference center was in a beautiful, mountainous location, but over an hour away from any hospital. The doctor warned that if I miscarried and hemorrhaged, my life would be in danger and, therefore, I should cancel my travel plans. I am not one that believes I should tempt the Lord by making valiant decisions that disregard obvious risks. Nor do I want to cower at risks or be led by fear, so my husband and I prayed together.

The theme of the retreat was based on the life of Esther. I was given four sessions to cover the book that never mentions God once, yet has His omnipotent, sovereign hand over all His children in the midst of their life-threatening circumstances. One of the most notable, pivotal responses Esther said in the face of danger was, "If I perish, I perish" (Esther 4:16). And after much prayer, this seemed to be the answer I was getting from the Lord, and Scott felt he should release me to go.

I knew halfway into the retreat that the power of God was moving on the hearts of the women, and that the life within my womb was leaving. No matter how much progesterone I took, the fight for the baby was over, and the bleeding grew worse. During the third session, it seemed appropriate that I should share with the women about the miscarriages I had previously, and the one I was currently having. By the grace of God, I was able to share of my unshakable faith—that no matter what He has allowed to hit my life, there was a peaceful place of surrender I had finally come to where I trust Him, and the pain of life (and death) was not going to separate me from His love. I believed in my heart I was supposed to come to the retreat, so the outcome was His allowance. I could not share that I understood His purpose, but I often prayed Job's words in Job 23:10: "But He knows the way I take; When He has tried me, I shall come forth as gold."

After the session was over, I could not believe how many women came forward and wanted to share about their own losses. One woman was a pastor's wife who had become so bitter over her miscarriage that she had not spoken to the Lord for five years. She had buried her brokenness and disguised her estrangement from the Lord to the congregation, but now wanted to make things right with Him again. It seemed to me that out of one small life being taken, I was able to watch many women resurrected as they got their hearts right with God.

When I got home there were many complications, and I did end up hemorrhaging in a hospital emergency room. Physical healing did not come quickly, but peace was more real to my soul than the mattress I lay on for many days.

Once my health improved, I had to go back to the maternity ward for the dreaded RhoGAM shot. I was so thankful that the silence of my waiting was not broken by newborn cries. I came home, tore off the bandage from my arm, and sat on the end of my bed, looking out the window in a daze. The lyrics to Horatio Spafford's hymn, "It is Well with My Soul" began to sing their words across my thoughts, and my heart echoed the words.

> *When peace, like a river, attendeth my way,*
> *When sorrows like sea billows roll;*
> *Whatever my lot, Thou hast taught me to say,*
> *It is well, it is well with my soul.*

Though Satan should buffet, though trials should come,
Let this blest assurance control,
That Christ hath regarded my helpless estate,
And hath shed His own blood for my soul.

But, Lord, 'tis for Thee, for Thy coming we wait,
The sky, not the grave, is our goal;
Oh, trump of the angel! Oh, voice of the Lord!
Blessed hope, blessed rest of my soul!

And Lord, haste the day when the faith shall be sight,
The clouds be rolled back as a scroll;
The trump shall resound, and the Lord shall descend,
Even so, it is well with my soul.

I remembered Horatio's story. After he had tragically lost a son, then nearly all of his wealth in the Chicago fire of 1871, he sent his wife and four young daughters to England to see Dwight Moody and Sankey in 1873. Midway across the Atlantic, their ship collided with another vessel and sank. A telegram was sent back to Horatio from his wife, "Saved alone." In the midst of overwhelming grief, he penned this legendary hymn to the Lord. I couldn't even imagine their devastation.

I stopped singing and prayed, "Lord, again, I can sit beside one or stand in front of many and testify to the reality that You are good. You do all things well, despite an enemy that is ruthless, a world that is worthless, and my flesh that opposes everything godly. I know You better than I ever have, and I'm so thankful. But my God, could you please give me a testimony of the 'power of your resurrection' from my life verse? I know it means more than salvation. I am so tired of death. Death around me and death within me. Please…show me…teach me."

I had no idea how God would answer that prayer, nor if He would, to be honest. But it wouldn't be long before an answer came that I never expected.

CHAPTER TEN

From Graves to Glory

Vance Havner, one of America's most beloved and oft-quoted preachers, once said, "When you cannot trace God's hand, you can trust His heart." Pain is one of the biggest clouds that conceals the Father's love for us. The deeper the pain, the deeper the attack upon trust.

And though time passed and grace was given for the day, despite the laughter in moments and love for friends and family, there was still a small, hidden stream of sorrow that flowed beneath it all.

One morning I woke to find my Bible reading that day was from John 11. The story of Jesus' friend, Lazarus, who had died and was resurrected back to life. I read the familiar pleadings of his sisters, Mary and Martha, "Lord, if You had been here, my brother would not have died." And once again, I marveled at the love of Jesus that purposely did not go to Lazarus when he was sick. My heart fought against echoing the sister's words, because I knew that Jesus was with me. I knew His love would respond to my pleadings in various ways, and I wouldn't always like it. But when I read that Jesus groaned and sighed in anger at the effects of sin and the pain it brought to people's lives, some sense of comfort blanketed a patch of my heart that was angry at death.

Then I read a familiar verse that seemed as though I had never seen it before. Jesus asked concerning Lazarus, "Where have you laid him?" God was asking the grievers to show Him where their dead friend was lain. Then a voice penetrated my thoughts, "Shannon, show Me where your dead lie."

I sat straight up on the couch and nearly threw my coffee. The question came again, encased with tenderness, but I shoved it aside and hurried off to the shower. A young lady was moving into our guest room soon, and I didn't have time for tears.

Though I knew better than to run from the Lord, His request echoed intentionally into my soul, "Shannon…show…Me…where YOUR dead lie." Though I've never heard an audible voice, there's an unmistakable voice that has become undeniable over the years.

I responded with pleading vulnerability, "Why, Lord? Babies and family and friends can't be resurrected like Lazarus!"

Then I saw a vision in my mind of a large, open field with sepulchers and graves dug throughout the rolling, grassy hills. In my thoughts, I walked up to each one with the Lord and said, "This is my dad. He died two months after he became the father I craved all my life when his pride was broken by cancer. This one is my stepdad, who was more of a father to me than my own dad was. This is my first baby, the one I lost before I knew I was pregnant. These are the twins…" and as my tears cascaded into a waterfall, I shut the spout off in the shower and got out.

While I wept into my towel, the vision grew so strong that I could not escape it. I watched, as one by one, powerful rays of light shot out with unbelievable force from the graves and tombs where all "my dead lie." Then in my mind, I heard similar words that Martha heard from Jesus in John 11:40: "Didn't I tell you that if you would believe, you would see the glory of God?"

My heart's defenses fell, and His gentleness caused me to see the vision of light coming from my stepfather's tomb. "Shannon, how many times have you shared the glorious testimony of how Bob was drawn to Me in the midnight hours and mercifully came to believe the Gospel just months before his life was over? From his death, didn't your mother come to salvation with relatives and friends hearing the gospel at his funeral?"

The rays from the next sepulcher caught my attention, "Remember how you found your sister's unopened letter with My name on the front that revealed her faith and prayer requests not long before I brought her home also?"

He continued to rehearse how He brought life and light, from death and darkness, all the while echoing the words, "If you will believe, you will see the glory of God."

When His words to my thoughts stopped, I looked over at tombs and graves where shadows still dwelt. I knew it was only an issue of trust and time, because He promised in Romans 8 and 11 that all things would work together for my good and His glory. Somehow, even the most tragic circumstances that Satan is allowed to carry out will be turned for a testimony of the glory and goodness of God.

Over the next few years, there were several hard circumstances that hit my life, yet each ended in such a way as to illustrate the power of His resurrection. I could sit down with anyone today and say that my God has fulfilled His promise from Isaiah 51:3, "The LORD will comfort Israel again and have pity on her ruins. Her desert will blossom like Eden, her barren wilderness like the garden of the LORD."

The fulfillment has not come from anyone being added to our family, our home, the church, or an increase in anything touchable. Instead, it has come in the way that the Lord has magnified Himself in normal, uneventful days. My brokenness has brought a dependency on the Word of God that reflects Job's words in Job 23:12 (NASB), "I have treasured the words of His mouth more than my necessary food."

It has come through the loosening of my grip on things that are temporary with a tenacious embrace of things that are eternal. It is the final realization that heaven is not nearly as distant as it always seemed to be, nor the Father's love as conditional as it used to feel. I could not even recount how the Lord changed the depth of my soul's convictions of what is most important and precious versus trifles and shallow concerns.

I have very little understanding about the ways of God, but I have surrendered to the truth of His words in Isaiah: "For my thoughts are not your thoughts, neither are your ways my ways, declares the LORD. For as the heavens are higher than the earth, so are my ways higher than your ways and my thoughts than your thoughts." I don't know how many times I shake my head in wonder, confused by tragedies that happen, but no longer fall back on the question,

"Lord, why did You…?" Only He knows how many times I have falsely accused Him of suffering and trials in life that Satan authored, engineered, then snickered as he stayed camouflaged and the Lord got the blame.

Death was not the Father's desire, nor is it His delight today. Sin was not His plan, it was man's choice. The Bible says of God, "Righteous and true are Your ways," and one day when we know the behind-the-scenes story of every event, we will marvel at the beauty of His character, the tenacity of His love, the endurance of His faithfulness, and the mercy woven throughout history. He promises in Psalm 25:3 (KJV) that no one who hopes or trusts in Him will ever be put to shame. "This hope we have as an anchor of the soul, both sure and steadfast…"

The year before my mother-in-law died, she often quoted this passage about the dandelion from Lilias Trotter's "Parables of the Cross." I didn't fully understand it at first, but now I've come to pray that this is true of my life.

Measure thy life by loss and not by gain,
Not by the wine drunk, but by the wine poured forth,
For love's strength standeth in love's sacrifice,
And he who suffers most has most to give.

"He who suffers most has most to give."

Epilogue

It was one of the most heated arguments I'd had in a long time. If the furious shouting in my head would have come out of my mouth, a quarter of the village I lived in would have heard it and dialed 911. My argument was factual and undeniable, but my body objected regardless of the evidence. I laid out the case that I needed to care for my dangerously sick child and husband, pay bills, answer emails, make phone calls, and run errands, but my flu-ridden body responded with its own fever pitch of pain and paralyzing weakness. As long as I could remember, I had never known this level of agony with the flu before.

"Mommy? Can I just lay next to you and you hold me?" My little girl's raspy voice interrupted my frustration, and she proceeded to wiggle down next to me through the top of my blanket. As she pulled my arm over her like a seat belt, I almost cried out from the movement. Athlete that I was, I bit my lip, held my tongue, and then noticed that she was wheezing in her chest and hotter than earlier. Last time I checked, her temperature hovered over 103 degrees.

As my love gently enfolded her fragility, I fought the unwelcome fear that always comes when I hear her struggle for breath. It's not that I replay the circumstances of her birth and how near to death she came. I don't rehearse the stories of others I know who have lost their children to sickness or disease. But I realize now that nearly every time I've been exposed to such horrible tragedies, they've left a deep impression in the back of my mind subtitled "possibility." And when painful possibilities fight their way to the forefront of my attention, they seem to grow in size and power and try to suffocate my faith.

As my own fever began to rise, every joint in my body felt inflamed and every muscle felt torn and bruised to the bone. With every cough that echoed my daughter's, came a hammer-like blow to my head, and I'd wince. I thought, "If I can barely tolerate this, my poor little girl…" and as I held her close, I began to weep for all she was going through, realizing I was feeling her pain as never before.

Then my thoughts lifted to what we would be celebrating that coming Friday—"Good Friday," we call it. That day, nearly two thousand years ago, when Jesus would embrace a depth of pain that no human being on earth had ever, nor will ever, experience. The impressions of suffering I had in my mind were incomparable to the impressions that human whips left across Jesus' flayed back. The seeming hammer that pounded my head was utterly inferior to the thorns that punctured Christ's skull. The wheezing I heard from my daughter reminded me of Jesus needing to push Himself up on the nail that pierced through his foot bones just so He could inhale the stench of the sin-filled atmosphere. The darkness that accompanied this sickness was near light in contrast to the touchable black horror that covered the earth for three hours while Jesus hung on the cross.

Isaiah 52 and 53 took on new understanding for me and I saw the correlation made in Hebrews 4 regarding Jesus as our High Priest. If I would weep because I felt a portion of the pain my daughter was feeling, how much more is our Savior moved with compassion for us when we walk through suffering and difficulty? He experienced the fullness of all of life's "possible" wounds; He felt more sorrow than any human would ever wallow in; He bore the weight of Satan's heaviest afflictions; and He drank empty the cup of God's wrath against sin so no one else would ever have to experience it. I am never alone one second of my day because Jesus took all of the Father's rejection and was forsaken in my place.

I listened as my daughter breathed heavy in sleep, thankful she found peace and rest while I held her. I prayed for her health and wholeness and for life to return to this vivacious little girl. Then I easily envisioned the heart of my Father, who is so perfect in His love that He would graciously give me a glimpse into His own heart that craves the same for me—peace and rest in His embrace. I would never think that I could love stronger as a parent than He does, yet I continually forget this truth when I don't see myself as His child.

He has always known where it hurts. He has understood every wince. He has heard every cry on a park bench, behind the wheel of a car, down a hospital corridor, and has collected every teardrop that has fallen down one of His kids' cheeks and pooled in their ear at night. He still translates our moans into heavenly requests and surrounds us with echoes of the promise, "If you will believe...you will see the glory of God." He has gone before us into our tomorrows and wants us to learn the habit of turning our attention from the fear of "possibilities" to the limitless treasure chest of "grace" to help us in our time of need. In those moments, the Holy Spirit will whisper straight into your soul, "Come to Me, you weak and weary child, and I will give you rest" (Matthew 11:28).

And within minutes, His peace tucked me in, His Presence filled my heart, and I fell asleep in the invisible, yet very real arms of the Lord.

For further reading, see Romans 5:12-21; 1 Corinthians 15:21, 26; Romans 6:23, and Revelation 21:4.

Shannon invites you to stay in contact with her in the following ways:

Blog: You can visit the author's blog at http://aquietplaceofgrace.org to read further reflections she's posted the last several years, download free resources, free images with scriptures, listen to and download Bible studies, and more.

Photography: One of the author's favorite hobbies is photography. She has an Instagram account under the name "itsnotgalatian," as well as a site to sell some of her work at https://alabaster-images.smugmug.com

Twitter: You can follow her by searching the name "ShanGallatin."

Email: If you'd like to make further contact privately, you can email "aquietplaceofgrace@gmail.com." Depending upon life's circumstances, she will respond as best she can.

ORDER INFORMATION

To order additional copies of this book, please visit
www.redemption-press.com.
Also available on Amazon.com and BarnesandNoble.com
Or by calling toll free 1-844-2REDEEM.

CPSIA information can be obtained
at www.ICGtesting.com
Printed in the USA
BVOW08s0931140917
494770BV00001B/1/P